Lower Your Expectations (and Other Life Skills)

Lower Your Expectations (and Other Life Skills)

Katie Simpson

Disclaimer

This book is intended for entertainment purposes only. The opinions, stories, and observations expressed are based on personal experiences and perspectives. While humor and sarcasm are used throughout, nothing in these pages should be taken as professional, medical, legal, or financial advice.

Names, details, and identifying characteristics may have been changed to protect privacy. Any resemblance to real persons, living or dead, is coincidental.

Readers are encouraged to laugh, reflect, and enjoy but please remember this book is not a substitute for professional guidance.

Dedication

To Ken. You are my calm, my chaos, my steady place. You've taught me more about patience, kindness, and unconditional love than you'll ever realize. I adore you, even when you steal my shampoo and conditioner. You make me laugh even when I want to scream, and that's true love.

Acknowledgments

To the everyday irritations that kept me inspired, thank you. Without bad drivers, shopping cart abandoners, reply-all warriors, and toxic bosses, this book wouldn't exist. You annoyed me into productivity.

To my friends who laughed at my drafts and said, "This is insane, but it's also true," you kept me going when I wondered if anyone else would find my world as ridiculous as I do.

To the readers: thank you for picking this up. If you laughed, nodded, or muttered "same" under your breath, then my job here is done. You're proof that we're all just trying to survive the mess together, one eye roll at a time.

And finally, to donuts, and diet Coke—you deserve royalties. You kept me upright, sarcastic, and sane enough to finish this book.

Preface

When I started writing this book, I thought it would simply be a collection of funny stories; little observations about life, people, marriage, aging, and the chaos of being human. But somewhere between the laughter, the irritation, the hot flashes, and the endless laundry, I realized I was writing something much deeper.

This book is a permission slip.

A permission slip to let go of perfection. To breathe. To slow down. To expect less from the world and more from the moments that matter. To be kinder to yourself and to others. To stop sprinting through life like you're being timed. To laugh at the ridiculousness of it all.

Life is heavy enough. The expectations placed on us, by society, by strangers, by ourselves, are unbearable if we carry them all at once. And yet we do. We try. We bend. We break. We fall apart quietly while pretending we're fine.

So I wrote this book as a gentle reminder. You don't have to keep up. You don't have to do it all. You don't have to be perfect.

Lower your expectations of the things that don't matter. Raise your appreciation for the things that do.

And somewhere along the way, you might just find peace. Not the loud, dramatic kind, but the soft kind that slips into your life quietly when you're finally still enough to notice it.

This is my story, my humor, my truth, and my heart.
I hope it meets you where you are.

Author's Note

This book was written during a season of clarity in my life. A season where I realized that rushing, performing, and trying to meet every expectation was slowly draining the joy out of my days. I needed to step back. I needed to breathe. I needed to remind myself that being human is hard enough without acting like I'm auditioning for the role of "Perfect Woman in a Perfect World."

If you're reading this, I want you to know something. You are not behind. You are not failing. You are not supposed to have it all together. You are not meant to survive on stress and self-criticism.

You're human. Beautifully, messily, imperfectly human.

And that's enough.

Wherever this book finds you; in chaos, in transition, in healing, in exhaustion, or simply in need of a laugh, I hope it gives you what you need. Even if it's just the comfort of knowing you aren't alone.

Thank you for being here. Thank you for reading my words. Thank you for letting me share my heart, scars, and sarcasm with you.

~Katie

Table of Contents

Chapter 1: Slow Down, You're Moving Too Fast

When I was a kid, life moved at the speed of real time. Not "5G real time," not "instant download," not "tap a button and summon tacos in 12 minutes" real time. I'm talking about slow, analog time. The kind where waiting was normal and absolutely no one died from it.

We had three channels on TV. Three. And if the president came on interrupting the show you'd been excited about all week? Tough luck. You were about to learn something about foreign policy whether you liked it or not.

There was no DVR, no binge-watching, no autoplay. You missed it? You missed it. Gone forever, like the last cookie in a house full of teenagers.

And remote controls? Please. *I* was the remote. My parents would bark, "Turn it to channel 2," and off I went, crossing the living room like a loyal retriever learning new commands. You got your steps in without ever trying.

We didn't have phones glued to our hands. No constant notifications telling us we're behind on emails, behind on news, behind on everyone else's curated lives. We weren't accessible 24/7 to every person with a thumb and a Wi-Fi signal.

Life was slower. Simpler. Quieter. And because of that… dare I say… easier.

Fast-forward to today, and everything is on demand.

Hungry? DoorDash.
Curious? Google.
Bored? Stream it.

Want groceries, a new wardrobe, and seasonal throw pillows? Click-click-click — all delivered before you can find your wallet.

Convenient? Yes. But here's the part nobody talks about. The faster life gets, the less we actually live it.

We are stretched thin, overstimulated, underjoyed, and multitasking like it's an Olympic sport. We expect everything instantly because everything is designed to be instant, which means anything that isn't instant feels like a personal insult.

Patience evaporates. Peace evaporates. And people wonder why we're all one slow walker away from losing our religion.

Modern life has turned us into on-demand humans. Everything we want, we get. But everything we get costs us attention, stillness, and the ability to breathe in the moment.

And somewhere inside all that noise, I learned something important. Just because the world moves fast doesn't mean you have to.

There is no rule that says you must keep up with everyone else's pace. You can actually (brace yourself)…slow down. You can live in the moment. The *actual* moment. Not the one you're racing toward. Not the one you're trying to capture for Instagram. The one you're standing in.

Because life's biggest miracles? They don't show up with fireworks. They don't make grand entrances with announcements from the

Universe. They don't come wrapped in neon signs saying, "HEY! HERE IS YOUR BREAKTHROUGH!"

Most miracles whisper. Most blessings arrive quietly. Most answers show up disguised as extremely ordinary moments.

But you have to be moving slowly enough to notice them.

Let me tell you a story.

A few years ago, I was between jobs and absolutely drowning in stress. I'd been laid off for nearly a year. My unemployment had long since run out. My savings account was gasping for air. And I had applied to *thousands* of jobs. Literally thousands. Nothing. Crickets. Just me, my laptop, and the kind of anxiety that eats your insides for breakfast.

One day, I was heading into town and stopped to get gas. Nothing symbolic. Nothing emotional. Just a routine "put fuel in the car so I can pretend I have somewhere important to be" moment.

While I stood there watching the pump numbers climb, I got this strong feeling — not a thought, not a worry — a feeling that I needed to go home.

Immediately. No errands. No "just one stop." Go home.

Of course, being human, I argued with myself. "Am I overthinking?" "Is this intuition or indigestion?" "Is this a warning from the Universe or am I just being dramatic?"

So naturally, I called Ken. Because when all else fails, call the man who has survived years of my intuition, my instincts, and my existential panics.

He didn't hesitate. He said, "If your gut is talking, listen to it. Go home."

So I did. Still doubting myself. Still wondering if I was being ridiculous. But I turned around and drove home.

I had barely walked through the door when my phone rang. A potential employer was on the other end, calling out of the blue, to see if I could interview in one hour.

If I had been on the road — even ten minutes farther from home — I would have missed that call. Missed that interview. Missed that opportunity. Missed the blessing I had been begging the universe for.

I got the job. A life-changing job. A stabilizing job. The job that ended that entire season of fear and uncertainty.

A miracle. Delivered in silence. Wrapped in intuition. Disguised as a random moment at a gas pump.

That day taught me something that stuck. Miracles rarely shout. They whisper. And if you're moving too fast, you'll miss them.

So no, I don't want to live at the speed of the internet anymore. I want to live at the speed of being human.

I want to taste my food. I want to watch sunsets without photographing them like an unpaid influencer. I want to sit with Ken and laugh without the soundtrack of notifications buzzing like angry insects.

More than anything, I want to give myself permission to lower the expectations that keep me stressed, distracted, and disconnected.

Life may be fast. But peace is slow. And I choose peace every time.

Chapter 2: Why Is Laundry Out To Get Me?

In my world, chaos doesn't always start with drama. Sometimes it starts with laundry piles large enough to qualify as structural hazards. We're not a family of six. We don't run a bed-and-breakfast. Yet somehow the mountain of clothes in the corner looks like we're auditioning for a reality show called *America's Next Top Laundromat Disaster.*

And it's not like we're fashion icons. My wardrobe is basically the same rotation of five "good" shirts, two pairs of jeans, and one dress I regret every time I put it on. Ken is even simpler. The man has mastered the minimalist uniform: five pairs of Wrangler jeans, five Carhartt shirts, and flannel when the temperature drops below 60. He could pack for a month-long trip in a grocery sack. Together, we barely qualify as people who produce enough laundry to justify a hamper.

Yet the laundry says otherwise.

Towels are the real villains. They multiply like rabbits. Bath towels, hand towels, dish towels…I don't even remember *using* half the towels that show up in the hamper. Every time I turn around, another damp towel materializes like it teleported in from a parallel universe. I swear we're running a secret towel testing lab without knowing it.

And the socks? Oh the socks. They vanish into another dimension. I put two in, I get one out. At this point, I'm convinced the dryer is powered entirely by mismatched socks. It eats them for energy like some kind of cotton-fueled furnace.

Some people swear laundry is "therapeutic." They put on music, fold everything neatly, organize drawers, and talk about the soothing smell of lavender fabric softener. I'm convinced these people are either liars or cult recruits. For the rest of us, laundry isn't therapy, it's quicksand. The more you do, the deeper you sink. You finish one load and feel proud for 12 seconds before discovering another mountain forming behind you like your hamper is mocking you with slow, sarcastic applause.

And the folding. Lord, the endless folding.

Let's talk about fitted sheets.

Whoever invented fitted sheets is absolutely on the wrong side of history. They do not fold. They *refuse* to fold. I've watched those YouTube tutorials where tidy people turn fitted sheets into perfect squares, and I'm convinced sorcery is involved. My personal method? Ball it up like a fabric meatball, shove it into the closet, and slam the door before it springs back out at me like an overly aggressive jack-in-the-box.

One time, Ken decided to "help" with the laundry. Bless his heart. He proudly announced he'd saved time by mixing everything, colors, towels, jeans, and of course, my favorite white shirt. What came out of that washer looked like a tie-dye experiment performed by a blindfolded raccoon. I thanked him, of course, because marriages are built on kindness… but he's been permanently banned from doing laundry ever since.

Every once in a while, I get ambitious. I swear this will be the week I stay ahead of the laundry. I'll do a little every day. I'll keep it manageable. I'll stay on top of it like the adult I allegedly am.

That lasts about… three days. Because then real life shows up. Work deadlines, errands, family drama, and the very realistic desire to sit down occasionally. Suddenly the laundry is back in the corner, multiplying, smirking at me, probably whispering, "Nice try, sweetheart."

I've come to accept that the laundry is going to outlive me. One day, archaeologists will excavate my house and find layers of towels and socks like geological sediment.

I've come to realize laundry is a lot like life.

It never really gets "done." It keeps coming whether you're ready or not. And perfection? Forget it. Laundry doesn't reward perfectionists. Laundry rewards survivors.

I've decided I've got better things to do, like lowering my expectations and hiding the last cookie from Ken.

And honestly? Maybe that's the lesson. Stop expecting the pile to shrink. Stop expecting life to be tidy. Stop expecting everything to stay folded in perfect little squares.

Because life, like laundry, is messy, relentless, and sometimes ridiculous. But at least it makes for a good story.

Chapter 3: Life's Greatest Mysteries

Forget the pyramids, the Bermuda Triangle, or Stonehenge. Those are amateur mysteries. The real enigmas, the ones that defy logic, physics, and the will to live, are happening right inside my own house.

Take Ken, for example.

The man is bald. Smooth-head bald. He has a scalp so shiny you could use it to signal aircraft in an emergency. And yet somehow, he uses my expensive shampoo and conditioner. Why? What exactly is he conditioning? His hope? His dreams? His scalp's emotional well-being?

When I ask him, he just shrugs like I'm the one being weird. Meanwhile, I'm watching a $60 bottle of salon conditioner disappear down the drain for absolutely no reason other than habit. That, my friends, is one of life's most unsolved and unnecessary mysteries.

Then there's the remote control. It has one job, to stay near the TV. One. But every day, without fail, it vanishes like it's joined the witness protection program. I've found it under couch cushions, in the bathroom, inside my car, and once in the refrigerator (don't ask).

Nobody ever admits to moving it. The remote just relocates itself like it's testing our sanity, slipping away at night to go clubbing with the lost socks.

Speaking of socks, seriously, where the hell do they go? I put two in the machine. ONE comes out. Somewhere there's a sock dimension. A magical land full of lonely, mismatched cotton souls living their best lives without us.

21

And while we're talking about real-world mysteries, let's talk about "overnight shipping." It never arrives overnight. Ever. I've paid extra for "overnight" packages that took a three-state sightseeing tour before wandering onto my porch three days late. Meanwhile, the tracking says things like "in transit" or "arriving soon." My package has been "in transit" longer than some relationships.

Here are more mysteries that keep me up at night.

Pens. Where do the good ones go? I have a drawer full of pens that don't work, but the single pen that writes beautifully is ALWAYS gone. Probably eloped with the dryer socks.

Easy-open packaging. Nothing "easy" about it. You need a blowtorch, a hacksaw, and possibly a small prayer circle to open a plastic clamshell. And five band aides to clean up the carnage.

Grocery store staffing. Ten checkout lanes. Three cashiers. Every. Single. Time.

Ken's blanket situation. Why does he need six blankets at night? What climate is he living in? And why do we share one bed but exist in two separate weather systems?

The point is, life is full of small mysteries that no scientist is ever going to solve. Nobody's getting a grant to figure out the sock-eating dryer conspiracy. No research team is investigating the migratory habits of remote controls. Amazon's certainly not updating its honesty policy on "overnight shipping."

Maybe the goal isn't to solve these mysteries at all. Maybe the secret is learning to laugh at them.

Because when you stop fighting life's weirdness and start seeing it for the comedy it is, everything gets a little lighter.

In our house, that means accepting that Ken will keep conditioning his bald head like it's a rare orchid. The remote will continue its nomadic lifestyle. Socks will disappear into the abyss. And packages will arrive when they feel like it.

And honestly? As long as we're laughing at the chaos, even the dumb stuff, I think we're doing just fine.

Chapter 4: Public Etiquette 101 (aka How Not to Be a Jerk in Target)

You'd think basic decency in public wouldn't require a training manual, but every time I step into a store, I'm reminded that common courtesy is apparently an elective class half the population skipped.

Let's start with the classic offender. Shopping carts. It is not, I repeat, not that hard to walk the extra ten feet and put the cart back where it belongs (the disabled and elderly are exempt). Yet abandoned carts roam parking lots like free-range cattle. One rolls into your car, another blocks the one open parking spot, and someone else has to wrangle the herd while the guilty party drives off like they just saved a life.

You're not "too busy." You're not "in a rush." You're just creating chaos for the next human. I've started rounding up carts like I work at the store. I even help the store people round them up, cheering them on like a proud parent. Admiring their techniques and how they precisely push 400 carts back into the store without running anyone over. That's impressive.

Can we talk about speakerphone people? Why, in the name of all things holy, do people think the world needs to hear their phone call on full volume? Nobody cares about your cousin's bunion removal or your drama-filled dinner plans. If you want to broadcast your life, start a podcast. Otherwise, turn your volume down and spare us the trauma.

And while we're at it, let's discuss littering. Throw your trash away. Just... Throw. It. Away. You carried it in. You can carry it out. Leaving your fast-food masterpiece on the table like you're expecting a personal maid to materialize does not make you important. It makes you lazy.

And movie theaters? When did it become socially acceptable to leave popcorn on the floor, drink cups abandoned, candy wrappers shoved into seats like hidden landmines? The staff is already underpaid. They don't need to clean up the evidence of your snack crimes.

Then there's the checkout line circus. Cutting in front of people because you're "in a hurry"? Congratulations, so is everyone else. That's why we're all in the express lane clutching our items with dead eyes, praying to get out before we lose our last sliver of hope.

And since we're already here, let's talk about self-checkout. I didn't clock in. I don't work here. I have received exactly zero training on your janky machines, yet every time I'm herded into that area like a confused goat, something explodes. The light starts flashing like I'm trying to steal a pack of gum, and the robotic voice keeps repeating "ASSISTANCE NEEDED" as if I summoned a demon instead of scanning bananas. If I'm going to do the job of a cashier, a bagger, AND loss prevention, then I want a discount, a W-2, and maybe even a name badge (with glitter).

None of this is complicated. It's basic human decency. Hold the door. Let someone merge. Say thank you. Don't treat public spaces like your personal playground.

One time, I watched a woman cut in front of an elderly man in the checkout line. Didn't look at him. Didn't acknowledge him. Just bulldozed her items onto the belt like she was solving world peace. I let him go ahead of me and gave her a side-eye so sharp it could've sliced through her recycled tote bag.

Did it fix society? No. Did it make her rethink her choices for one hot second? Absolutely.

Ken, of course, would've handled it differently. He has the patience of a saint wrapped in Carhartt. He would've probably offered to bag her groceries just to shame her politely. I admire that kind of composure. Unfortunately, I have to bite my tongue and hope I don't accidently say what I'm thinking out loud.

Public etiquette is really just the golden rule with a shopping cart. Treat people how you want to be treated. Not because it's profound. Not because it'll change the world overnight. But because the world is exhausting enough already.

Returning your cart isn't going to solve world hunger. Not yelling at someone in traffic won't end global warming. Cleaning up your table won't cure diseases.

But it DOES make the day easier for the next exhausted human trying to survive the chaos.

Which is kind of the whole point. Lower your expectations of people, raise your standards of kindness, and for the love of all that's decent... don't be an obstacle disguised as a human.

Moments like that remind me that kindness doesn't have to be loud to be powerful. Sometimes it's just choosing not to make someone else's day harder.

Chapter 5: Customer Service Roulette

Calling customer service is basically emotional gambling. You dial that number knowing full well the odds are not in your favor, but you still hope, naïvely, that maybe, just maybe, you'll hit the jackpot and reach someone who actually knows what they're doing.

Here how it usually goes. First, you dial. Then the automated menu begins its assault. "Press one for English. Press two if you'd like to scream. Press three to repeat these options while questioning all your life choices."

Then comes the robotic voice claiming, "I'm sorry, I didn't get that." Of course you didn't robot machine. You never do. You were programmed for suffering.

By the time you finally reach a human being, you've already entered your account number, date of birth, address, the last four digits of your DNA, and the blood type of your childhood hamster, only for the representative to cheerfully say, "Can I get your account number?"

Customer service reps fall into two categories. The first are angels disguised as humans. They speak so you can understand them. They fix your problem in five minutes flat. You want to send them a fruit basket. You'd name your next child after them. You hang up with renewed optimism for life.

The second category are agents of pure chaos. The answer the phone in very broken English and you darn well know they are not named "Mary" in real life. You explain your problem. They put you on hold. They come back and act like they're speaking to you for the very first time. It's customer service Groundhog Day.

Let's talk about the hold music. That tinny, looping elevator track that sounds like someone recorded three sad keyboard notes in 1994 and called it good. If you're really lucky, the music cuts out completely and leaves you in dead silence. This is the psychological equivalent of dangling over a cliff.

Do you hang up? Do you wait? Are you still in a queue? Are you even alive anymore? Nobody knows.

I once spent over an hour on hold for an internet issue. By the time a human picked up, I had forgotten why I even called. I'd had 45 minutes to spiral through every problem in existence, so when the rep finally said, "How can I help?" I launched into a rant combining my internet bill, global warming, and the price of avocados.

Their solution? "Try unplugging the router." Yep, already did that three times prior to calling. Why do you think I'm calling?

Ken finds all of this hilarious. Anytime I'm on hold pacing the living room like a caged jungle cat, he strolls by with his iced tea and says, "They'll get to you right after they solve world peace."

He thinks he's funny. He's not wrong, but still.

And then there's the customer-service chatbot. The little pop-up that says, *Hi! I'm here to help!* No, you're not. You're here to misunderstand every question I ask and then direct me to the FAQ page like it's going to save my life.

Chatbot: "Did this answer your question?"
Me: "THIS IS A NIGHTMARE."

Chatbot: "Great! Connecting you with an agent!"
No one has ever felt so unseen.

I've also accidentally trauma-dumped on a customer service rep because the hold time gave me too long to think. There I was, venting about my interest rate increase and suddenly confessing my childhood fears. The poor guy just wanted to explain the reasons for the interest rates. He wasn't prepared for a therapy session. That's what happens when I have lots of time to think.

Customer service isn't about solving problems. It's psychological warfare. It's a patience exam disguised as a phone call.

Sometimes you win. Sometimes you lose. Sometimes you hang up, cancel your account, and decide you never needed Wi-Fi anyway.

That's customer service roulette. Spin the wheel. Pray for empathy. Try not to rage-eat an entire sleeve of cookies while you're on hold.

Most days, we're all just one inconvenience away from unraveling, and maybe the real victory is not letting small frustrations steal our whole peace.

Chapter 6: Social Media Is Not Therapy

Social media was supposed to be fun. A place for vacation photos, dog pictures, and maybe the occasional humblebrag about your kid winning the spelling bee. Instead, it's turned into an emotional landfill where people unload every thought, fight, and meltdown like they're auditioning for reality TV.

Your newsfeed is not a therapist's office. Posting vague status updates like, *"Some people know what they did"* isn't healing, it's confusing. Who are these "some people"? We need to know; don't leave us hanging. The rest of us are just trying to scroll past and find a funny cat video.

And let's be honest, oversharing doesn't fix anything. Posting every breakup detail, every family feud, or every time your neighbor's dog barked too loud doesn't solve the problem. It just gives everyone else something to screenshot.

I've fallen into the scroll spiral myself. One minute it's vacation photos, the next it's a political brawl, then a dog in sunglasses, followed by a live video of someone sobbing because their boyfriend ghosted them. Fifteen minutes later, I feel worse than when I started. It's like eating empty calories; you're full, but you're not satisfied. So I close the app, pour a glass of diet Coke, and have an actual conversation with Ken. Shocking, I know.

Shall we discuss Facebook pages? In my town, there's a page that's supposed to be about road conditions. Simple, right? Report on icy spots, accidents, and traffic so people can travel safely. In reality, it's turned into argument central. Someone reports a wreck, the next person blames the driver, and within five comments it's a full-blown political debate about whose fault snow is. At this point, I don't even check it for road conditions. I check it for entertainment. It's basically free reality TV with a side of weather updates. Grab your popcorn because someone's about to get banned.

The bigger problem is that social media has wrecked how people communicate. Folks can write a 500-word rant in a comments section but can't look their neighbor in the eye to have a real conversation. They'll threaten to "unfriend" someone online but can't handle basic disagreement in person. That's not connection, it's chaos dressed up with emojis.

Social media is addictive, not connective. Every "like" is a little dopamine hit, every angry comment is a tiny adrenaline rush. But none of it fills the actual void. That's why people post their meltdowns for strangers instead of picking up the phone and calling someone who actually cares.

Ken doesn't do social media. He says, "If people want to know what I'm doing, they can come over." Which is adorable until three of them actually do.

At the end of the day, social media isn't therapy. It's a public diary with better lighting and worse boundaries. Post your vacation pics, brag about your dog, show me your dinner if it involves cheese. But if you're about to type "some people need to learn respect," maybe close the app and call an actual friend instead. Your mental health (and the rest of us) will thank you.

We weren't built to carry the world's emotions at once, especially not through a glowing rectangle in our hands.

Chapter 7: Little Things That Drive You Nuts

It's not always the big stuff that breaks you. It's the tiny, everyday irritations that pile up until you're one slow walker away from snapping.

Patience isn't tested by life's major disasters. It's tested when you're behind someone paying with a check in 2025. It's tested when the grocery store scanner won't recognize your apple, when autocorrect insists you meant *"ducking,"* and when your keys vanish into a black hole right as you're running late.

Here's my personal highlight reel of offenders:

- **Reply-all warriors.** The people who think hitting reply-all to say *"Thanks!"* is necessary. Now 200 inboxes hate you.
- **Speakerphone oversharers.** Broadcasting their bunion surgery in the middle of Target like its breaking news. Nobody asked.
- **People watching YouTube videos at restaurants.** Seriously, we are trying to enjoy our meal in peace. We don't want to listen to your video on full volume.
- **Doorway blockers.** They stop dead in the middle of an aisle or doorway like human traffic cones. MOVE.
- **The loud chewers.** Crunching popcorn like it's their personal audition for a sound effects album.
- **Line cutters.** Always "didn't see" the 12 people ahead of them, but somehow spotted the cashier just fine.

Once, I tried to rise above it all. Deep breathing, mindfulness, the whole thing. Then a man in front of me at the gas station spent five minutes scratching ten lottery tickets at the counter. Enlightenment ended right there.

None of these things are world-ending, but they're enough to wreck your mood in the moment.

One day I was already late, couldn't find my keys, and ended up trapped behind the human embodiment of a Sunday stroll. No urgency, no blinker, just vibes. By the time I finally got where I was going, it wasn't even about that driver anymore. It was about the lost keys, the dumb emails, the pile of laundry waiting at home. That driver was just the straw that snapped the camel's back.

Ken's solution to these annoyances is simple: walk away. He'll abandon an entire grocery cart if the aisles are too clogged, no hesitation. Meanwhile, I'm stuck muttering under my breath like an exorcist-in-training, trying to hold it together. Together, we're a disaster. He leaves without the milk. I leave with high blood pressure.

Most of the time, it's not that one annoying moment that breaks us. It's the hundreds we never slowed down long enough to feel.

These little irritations aren't going anywhere. People will always abandon carts, chew loudly, and cut lines. If you expect perfect behavior from strangers, you'll lose your mind. Lower your expectations, laugh when you can, and mutter to yourself if you must.

The world's never going to run out of small annoyances, but we do get to choose our reaction. Laugh, mutter, pour wine, repeat. That's emotional cardio.

Chapter 8: Family, Friends, and Frenemies

Nothing brings out the best and worst in people faster than family, friends, and frenemies. These are the three groups who can bring you joy, migraines, and wine cravings, sometimes all before lunch.

Let's start with family. You don't choose them, but you're stuck with them. They can love you fiercely, support you when you need it, and also drive you absolutely insane. Family gatherings are proof that humans can survive war zones. And just because someone is "family" doesn't mean they get unlimited access to you. Boundaries aren't disrespect; they're survival. Sometimes the healthiest thing you can do is skip the holiday dinner and enjoy your mashed potatoes in peace.

I used to feel guilty about skipping things, like I was letting people down. Then I realized the only person I was really letting down was myself every time I forced myself into rooms that drained me.

Friends, on the other hand, are the family you actually get to pick. The good ones are priceless. The people you can laugh with until your stomach hurts, cry without embarrassment, and text at 2 a.m. without apology. A good friend will tell you when you're being ridiculous. A great friend will be ridiculous right next to you. Treasure those people. They're rare.

Then there are the frenemies. You know the type. They smile to your face but secretly root for your downfall. Their compliments come wrapped in question marks. *"Oh, I love your outfit… have you gained weight?"* They're suspiciously quiet when you succeed, but they'll broadcast your struggles like breaking news. Frenemies add drama to your life like seasoning, and you don't need that flavor.

And if you've ever sat through a holiday dinner with extended family, congratulations! You've already passed emotional survival training. You know how it goes. Within ten minutes, someone's lecturing about politics, someone else is passive-aggressively commenting on your life choices, and the cousin who just joined a pyramid scheme is handing out flyers like it's Black Friday. Meanwhile, Grandma is pouring wine like it's her Olympic event. Survival isn't about winning the argument. It's about making it to dessert without flipping the table.

Sometimes, though, family chaos creates epic comedy. When I was a kid, I sat through one of those tense family dinners where everyone was walking on eggshells. Out of nowhere, my grandmother (whom I dearly loved) looked at my father and announced she was going to start a business. He asked, "Why? What would you do at your age?" Without missing a beat, she said, "I'm going to open a fish bait shop and call it *The Masterbater.*" My father spit his food across the table, my grandfather kept eating like nothing happened, and I suddenly realized exactly where I got my wit from. Epic doesn't even cover it.

As I've gotten older, I've learned that protecting my peace isn't selfish. It's how I stay sane in a world full of emotional landmines.

As for me? I don't do drama. Period. If you're going to be in my life, the drama stays out. I'm all about friendships that uplift and inspire, not ones that drain me with gossip, backhanded comments, or constant chaos. Life is too short to babysit grown adults who thrive on stirring the pot. If someone can't bring honesty, humor, or at least peace to the table, they don't get a seat at mine.

The bottom line? Love your people. Invest in the good friends. Put up with the weird ones in small doses. And when it comes to frenemies? Stop feeding them. Nothing drives a frenemy crazier than realizing they don't matter.

Family, friends, frenemies; each one teaches you something. But the biggest lesson? Protect your peace. Lowering your expectations for people doesn't mean lowering your standards for love. It means protecting your peace like it's an heirloom.

Because in the end, it's not about who fills the room. It's about who fills your life with peace.

Chapter 9: Good Friends Are Hard to Find

Making friends as an adult is like dating without the wine. Awkward, complicated, and half the time, not worth the effort.

When you're a kid, friendship is easy. You sit next to someone in class, share a snack, and boom, you're best friends. As an adult, you can talk to someone for months before realizing the only thing you actually share is a mutual hatred of Mondays.

That's why good friends are rare. The kind who don't just hang around when it's convenient but genuinely make your life lighter. The ones who make you laugh until your stomach hurts, who tell you the truth even when you don't want to hear it, and who still show up when life gets messy. If you've got even one of those, you've hit the jackpot.

Adult friendships are weird. You're constantly walking the line between oversharing and "Did I say too much?"

You wonder if the other person is busy or just avoiding you.

You exchange twenty 'we need to get together soon!' messages before either of you actually commits.

You bond over shared trauma, exhaustion, and the understanding that we're all just doing our best not to lose our minds.

The rest? They're surface-level acquaintances. You smile, wave, maybe chat about the weather in the grocery store aisle, and move on. Nothing wrong with that but not everyone deserves a backstage pass to your life.

The problem is, as adults, we're often tricked into thinking friendship has to look like the movies. Girls' trips, endless brunches, picture-perfect squads. But that's not real life. Real friendship doesn't need to be polished. It's not about constant Instagram-worthy outings. It's about connection in the middle of the ordinary.

Some people will drain you with their chaos, drama, or endless one-sided conversations. Those aren't friends, they're unpaid therapy sessions. If you're going to be in my circle, you need to bring honesty, humor, and peace, not chaos. Friendship should lift you up, not wear you out.

Ken's philosophy on friendships is simple. "Friendships should feel like folding laundry with someone. It's still a chore, but somehow easier together." Honestly, I think he's right.

Life gets quieter and clearer when you stop chasing crowded rooms and start valuing the people who make you feel safe just by being themselves.

For me, my circle is intentionally small. Ken is my ride-or-die, my soft place to land, my favorite human, my best friend, and my comic relief. With him, I don't need to explain myself or compete. We laugh at the same ridiculous things, shake our heads at the same nonsense, and built a life where the best nights are the ones on the porch with a glass of sweet tea, not at some elaborate event we didn't want to attend anyway.

Lowering your expectations about friendship doesn't mean giving up. It means being honest. You don't need a crowd of people. You need a handful of people who truly get you. A friend who brings you coffee unasked, who shows up in sweatpants instead of dressing up for a "girls' night," who doesn't judge your messy house because theirs looks the same.

You don't need ten friends. You don't even need five. You need ones who are real, reliable, and willing to sit in the mess of life with you instead of standing on the sidelines offering "thoughts and prayers" while you drown.

Because when life gets hard, and it always does, you don't need a perfect friendship squad. Lower your expectations for quantity; raise them for quality. One honest friend beats ten brunch photos any day.

That's the joy of lowered expectations. Stop chasing the perfect friendship and start appreciating the imperfect ones that actually last.

Chapter 10: Marriage, Pedicures, and Other Surprises

Marriage is a lot of things. Partnership, chaos, laughter, compromise, and occasionally wondering why this person loads the dishwasher like a deranged raccoon. It's not perfect, but if you're lucky, it's the one place in life where you can be fully yourself—socks with holes, messy hair, questionable habits and all.

Forget the fairytales. Marriage isn't candlelit dinners and endless romance montages. It's inside jokes, bad habits, and loyalty so strong you'll run to the store at midnight because the other one *needs* ice cream immediately. It's not glamorous, but it's real. And that's what makes it work.

In my house, romance looks like cheap dinners eaten off paper plates. It looks like drinking from the hose after a long day, or riding the fence line together, looking for holes to repair. It's not roses and candlelight. It's being side by side, trying to figure it all out. It may not look romantic to the world's unattainable standards, but it's ours. And honestly, that's better.

And then there are the moments that are less "romantic comedy" and more "unintentional comedy." Like the time I told Ken I loved him, and without missing a beat, he replied, "I miss Olive Garden too." Was it heartfelt? Not exactly. Was it hilarious? Absolutely. Did we realize Ken may need hearing aids? Yes.

Marriage is also knowing your limits. For example, I am not allowed near the grill, the weed eater, or the tractor. Apparently my "enthusiasm" outpaces my coordination. And honestly? He's probably right. Every time I so much as look at the tractor, he gives me the same look people give toddlers hovering near the stovetop—equal parts love and sheer terror. That's partnership.

Of course, Ken has his quirks too. Take him to a hobby store with those giant craft letters, and suddenly he's spelling out things like *"My farts smell"* for the world to see. Try shopping with him, and it's like taking a toddler to try on clothes, whining, resistance, and then refusing to take off the one shirt he actually likes. At this point, I've learned to just let him buy his clothes at the local feed store. He is perfectly happy with five pairs of Wrangler jeans and five Carhartt T-shirts. Winter wear? Just add flannel. Problem solved.

And then there was the frozen yogurt incident. One Friday night, we decided to try a new shop in town. A group of girls outside were whispering and giggling when Ken strutted past them like a rooster, convinced he "still had it." Inside, they looked over again and said, "Isn't he cute? He reminds me of my grandpa." Deflation complete. Was it glamorous? Not even close. Was it romantic? In a weird way, yes, because we laughed about it together all night. That's marriage. It's being humbled together, side by side, and knowing you'll always have someone to laugh with.

Marriage isn't about looking perfect together. It's about finding someone who can laugh with you through every awkward, humbling moment life throws your way.

The real magic of marriage isn't in grand gestures. We started out thinking marriage meant grand gestures. Turns out, survival is romantic. It's fixing a fence in the rain, holding hands in a waiting room, laughing until one of us snorts. That's the good stuff. It's in friendship. It's in the little routines, the shared disasters, the inside jokes, and the everyday loyalty. It's about choosing each other, over and over, even when you're tired, annoyed, or knee-deep in chaos.

We may not have movie romance, but we have laughter, laundry, and tacos. And that's a love story worth keeping.

Chapter 11: The Magic of Saying No

Somewhere along the line, "no" became a dirty word. People act like saying it will shatter the universe, end friendships, or cause the PTA to collapse in flames. So instead, we tiptoe around it with soft maybes, long-winded excuses, or fake coughs into the phone.

Ken never struggles with this. If someone asks for something he's not up for, he suddenly remembers an urgent tractor emergency. I'm still studying that level of confidence.

Let me clear this up. *"No" is a complete sentence.*

You don't owe anyone a PowerPoint presentation on why you can't attend their candle party on a Tuesday night. You don't have to wrap your rejection in bubble wrap with three layers of apologies. No is enough.

But we're conditioned to feel guilty about it. We don't want to disappoint anyone. We don't want to look selfish. We don't want to miss out. So we say yes to things we hate, agree to commitments we don't have time for, and end up sitting in a folding chair wondering how we got roped into volunteering for a bake sale when we don't even bake.

The harsh reality? Every time you say yes when you mean no, you're signing a contract with resentment. And resentment charges interest. You'll sit there smiling through gritted teeth, handing out brownies you bought at the store, while silently plotting your escape from humanity.

Case in point. Our acquaintance once asked Ken and I to water his lawn while he was out of town. "No problem," we graciously agreed, knowing our free time was limited. We pictured a yard. A normal yard. Maybe a little hose-wrangling. Maybe ten minutes of our lives max. What he failed to mention was that his "lawn" was *five acres.* Five. Acres. You don't water a lawn like that. You irrigate it like you're auditioning to be a farmer. He even left us a four-wheeler to get around the property. That was the first red flag.

Ken, of course, thought this was the greatest thing ever. He was zipping around on the four-wheeler like he was starring in his own action movie while I was trying to figure out which lever turned on the sprinklers and which one opened the gates of hell. Somewhere between dragging hoses and swatting mosquitoes, I managed to fall headfirst straight into the irrigation ditch. Graceful, I know. Ken had to haul me out, laughing so hard he nearly fell in himself. I came out soaked, covered in weeds, and furious. He came out with the story of a lifetime. Our neighbor came home to a barely damp lawn and zero clue that I'd nearly drowned trying to keep his precious grass alive.

I was livid at the whole situation. Somewhere between the soaked jeans and mosquito bites, I realized I wasn't mad at the acquaintance. I was mad at myself for saying yes when I didn't want to. That's the fine print on people-pleasing. You end up resenting the wrong person.

That was the day I realized saying yes to things you don't actually want to do isn't generosity, it's stupidity dressed up as politeness. I should've just said no.

Life got lighter once I learned to use that word. Because saying no is freedom. It gives you back your time, your sanity, and your ability to sit on the couch guilt-free while everyone else is stuck in a committee meeting about paperclips.

Saying no doesn't make you selfish, lazy, or unkind. It makes you honest. And honesty is a lot kinder than pretending you're interested while secretly praying for a natural disaster to cancel the event.

So go ahead. Say no. Say it without guilt, without apology, without explanation. Protect your time. Protect your peace.

Lowering your expectations isn't giving up. It's giving yourself permission to stop drowning in obligations disguised as kindness.

Because the real magic of no is not about shutting people out. It's about keeping yourself whole. And sometimes, that's the only thing standing between you and total burnout.

Chapter 12: Kindness Isn't Hard

Kindness shouldn't be complicated. It doesn't cost money, doesn't require training, and no one needs a certification to master it. Yet somehow, people act like kindness is an Olympic-level skill reserved for elite athletes with excellent manners and perfect childhoods.

Holding a door. Saying thank you. Letting someone merge. These aren't grand gestures. They're the bare minimum of not being a jerk. But apparently, many folks missed that day in Human Decency 101.

Life is already hard enough. Between the bills, jobs, family drama, diets, lost keys, menopause, teenagers, dogs that bark at absolutely nothing. Why make it harder by being rude on top of it?

If you can be anything, at least aim for "slightly less difficult."

I've decided nothing tests humans more than driving. Some people are perfectly lovely on foot, but the minute they get behind the wheel, their soul leaves their body. Suddenly they're tailgating, swerving, speeding through no-passing zones, all while scrolling through their phone like they're auditioning for *Fast & Furious: Entitlement Edition.*

Meanwhile, Ken is the opposite. He waves at every car like he's in a parade. He smiles at strangers. He lets people merge with the enthusiasm of someone handing out puppies.

I, on the other hand, cuss more when driving than anywhere else. Between all the chaotic drivers making poor choices and the near missed accidents, my patience runs pretty thin.

Then there are doorway blockers, aisle hogs, and the grocery store Olympics. You know the ones. Stopped dead in the middle of the aisle, cart sideways, staring at the shelves like they're solving a math equation.

Do I get annoyed? Yes. Absolutely yes.

Do I fantasize about gently nudging their cart forward with my own like a bumper car? Also yes.

But then I remember, people are tired. People are overwhelmed. People are carrying invisible loads I can't see. And sometimes that "aisle blocker" is just a person trying to remember if they still have butter at home.

Kindness doesn't mean letting people walk all over you. One time at the grocery store, a woman held up the entire checkout line with her personal drama while the rest of us stood there aging. I quietly and kindly asked her to keep the line moving so the rest of us could check out.

Apparently, she took that as an invitation to scream like I'd insulted her ancestors. She went off like a fire alarm having an emotional episode. There I was, blinking at her like, "Ma'am, all I said was can you finish your transaction." Meanwhile, Ken was trying to wedge himself between us before it turned into a full-blown parking-lot showdown next to the rotisserie chickens.

But even then, even with her unhinged monologue echoing across aisle seven, I kept my voice soft. I didn't escalate. I didn't match her chaos. I didn't ruin her day more than she was already ruining it for herself.

Because kindness isn't weakness. And it sure as hell isn't silence. Kindness is choosing not to become the villain in someone else's story, even when they're *actively auditioning* for the role in yours.

Everyone's carrying something. That cashier you're snapping at? Could be their third double shift. That server you're judging? Might have been crying in the back five minutes ago. That grumpy stranger? Might be dealing with something you can't even imagine.

We don't know people's lives. We don't see their burdens. But we DO get to choose how we show up.

Being kind won't fix the world. It won't cure diseases. It won't make your boss less of a nightmare, stop traffic, or convince loud chewers to close their mouths.

But kindness DOES make the world softer. More livable. Less exhausting.

And honestly? With everything we're all going through, the absolute least we can do is not make life harder for one another.

Kindness isn't about perfection. It's not about sainthood. It's about choosing grace over rage, patience over ego, perspective over entitlement.

So the next time you feel like snapping? Take a breath. Put the cart back. Say thank you. Let someone merge. Speak gently. Lead with humanity.

It's not about being a saint. It's about not adding to the chaos.

And in a world this tired, that might be the kindest thing any of us ever do.

Chapter 13: The Weight That Won't Budge

One day you wake up, look in the mirror, and realize you've gained forty pounds—overnight. At least that's how it feels. You didn't suddenly start eating chocolate-covered cinnamon bears at midnight (well… not regularly, and they're only available during the holidays and I have standards). But somehow, your jeans are now gaslighting you, and your body has decided to store fat like it's prepping for the apocalypse.

At this stage of life, I swear I can gain weight just by looking at food. Forget eating the cake. If I so much as walk past a bakery and inhale too deeply, that's three pounds right there.

And the betrayal of clothes? Brutal. That pair of jeans that used to make you feel like a rockstar now feels like they're personally attacking you. We all like to tell ourselves they must have shrunk in the dryer. Let's be real, it's not the dryer. It's the damn bagel you looked at last Tuesday.

I once tried on half my closet in a desperate attempt to find something that fit. By outfit number six, I was sweaty, frustrated, and ready to set fire to the whole wardrobe. My husband, bless him, said, "You look great in all of them." Sweet, but also a blatant lie, because I could barely breathe in one of those pairs of pants. Love doesn't fix circulation.

At one point, I asked him point-blank if he still found me attractive with my menopause weight. He sat there for a moment (probably running through every possible answer, trying to decide if this was a setup and how not to die) and then said, "Yes, I do. I couldn't be married to a little tiny thing that can't lift feedbags." That's true love right there. Forget roses and candlelight. If your partner appreciates your ability to haul feed, you're golden.

The diet industry feeds off this misery. "Lose ten pounds in a week!" "Cut carbs and magically transform into a goddess!" Lies. All of it. I've lost and gained the same twenty pounds so many times I should get frequent flyer miles. Every new plan promises hope, and every plan ends with me cranky, hungry, and wondering how lettuce became my enemy.

The truth is sometimes the weight just won't budge. Not because you're lazy. Not because you lack willpower. Not because you don't care. Bodies change. Hormones shift. Stress piles on. And sometimes your metabolism just stages a full-blown protest.

Menopause is its own villain. Your body goes rogue. One day you wake up and the scale says, "New number, who dis?"

Your waistline becomes more of a suggestion than a measurement. And your thighs develop the uncanny ability to cling to calories like they're emotionally attached.

It's not you, it's hormones. And gravity. And life.

I'm just going to spell it out. Your worth is not measured in pounds. Your value is not tied to a clothing size. Your body is not failing you. It's adapting, surviving, carrying you through hell and back.

You are not less beautiful, less lovable, or less anything because your jeans are rude.

My body has carried me through everything, pain, joy, storms, miracles, and the least I can do is give it grace when it changes.

If stretchy pants are the uniform of middle-age survival? Then I proudly accept my warrior status.

Stretchy pants don't judge. They don't lie. They don't shame. They support you — literally and emotionally.

Lower your expectations of perfection. Raise your expectations of self-love.

The weight may not budge. But neither will your strength. Your humor. Your resilience. Your ability to show up in a world that expects women to shrink.

You don't need to shrink. You need to live.

Chapter 14: Diets Are a Scam (and Tacos Are Forever)

If I had a dollar for every diet I've tried, I could probably buy my own taco truck and live happily ever after. The diet industry is built on one thing: convincing you that you're broken.

You're not broken. You're just hungry.

Every diet promises a miracle. Meanwhile, I promise to keep believing tacos are a food group.

Keto will "transform your life." Juice cleanses will "reset your system." Intermittent fasting will make you glow. Cutting out bread will apparently turn you into a goddess.

I don't know about you, but cutting out bread just makes me homicidal.

The cycle is always the same:

- You start a diet with high hopes.
- You feel deprived within three hours.
- You cheat a little.
- You feel guilty.
- You swear to start again tomorrow.

Repeat until you're cranky, lightheaded, and convinced that lettuce is out to kill you.

And can we talk about the celebrities selling this stuff? You ever notice how the skinniest, most famous people always look a little… angry? Not moody-model "brooding." I mean flat-out pissed. It's because they're starving. They're not mad about paparazzi. They're mad because they haven't had a carb since 2012. That red-carpet scowl? Hunger. That "I'm better than you" look? Just them imagining you eating a cheeseburger. Honestly, I'd be cranky too if my dinner was five almonds and a sad green juice.

Meanwhile, tacos never lie. Tacos don't scowl at you. Tacos show up warm, loaded with cheese, and happy to see you.

And then there was the liquid shake diet incident. Oh, this one deserves a spot in the "what the hell was I thinking" hall of fame. The plan was simple: replace meals with shakes. Easy, right? Only what I didn't realize was that these particular shakes were loaded with caffeine. Like… a lot of caffeine.

But I was starving. STARVING. So naturally, instead of one shake, I drank three.

Within an hour, I wasn't just hungry. I was vibrating. My hands shook. My legs bounced. I couldn't sit still. I looked like a rabbit that had been mainlining espresso shots behind the garage. Ken walked in, took one look at me pacing the kitchen like a caged zoo animal, and said, "What the hell did you do?" At that point, I was convinced my heart was going to pound straight out of my chest and take off running without me.

I tried to lie down, but that made it worse. I just twitched like a malfunctioning robot. I ended up cleaning half the house in record time because sitting still was no longer an option. Basically, I became a Roomba with a pulse. Needless to say, that diet didn't last long.

Ken still brings it up whenever I'm "trying something new." His imitation of me vibrating through the kitchen could win awards.

I went back to tacos within 24 hours, mostly because tacos don't make you feel like you're auditioning for a speed-racing competition you never signed up for.

Food isn't the enemy. Joyless eating is. Life is too short to spend it counting almonds or pretending cauliflower rice is the same as real rice. (It's not. Stop lying.)

You don't need to pledge allegiance to some diet plan written by a man in a lab coat who's never met you. You need balance, honesty, and maybe a margarita.

Diets don't work long-term because they're not designed to. If they actually worked, the industry wouldn't be worth billions. They thrive on failure—your failure—so you'll keep buying shakes, powders, and miracle teas forever.

So here's my manifesto. Eat the damn taco. Eat two. Add extra cheese. Nobody's last words were ever, *"I wish I'd eaten more salad."*

Chapter 15: The Fixes That Don't Fix

We live in a world obsessed with "solutions." There's a product, a plan, or a program for every problem you've ever had. Stressed? There's a tea for that. Tired? There's a pill for that. Sad? There's a $300 course that promises to unlock your inner light through interpretive dance. None of it works.

Ken once asked if my 'detox tea' could unclog a drain. Honestly, it probably could have. The label said it removed toxins, but it mostly removed my will to live.

I can't even count the money I've wasted chasing "fixes." Powders that promised boundless energy. Serums that swore they'd erase ten years of wrinkles. Fitness gadgets that allegedly melt fat while you sit on the couch. Newsflash: I'm still tired, still wrinkled, and still staring at the same forty pounds that showed up overnight and refuses to leave.

The modern version of snake oil doesn't come out of the back of a wagon. It shows up on Instagram in sleek packaging with hashtags like #Wellness and #GlowUp. They tell you this powder will change your life. This retreat will heal your soul. This app will finally get you organized. And for a few weeks, you believe it. You drink the chalky powder, light the overpriced candles, and download the rainbow-colored calendar app. And then you're right back where you started, but now with a lighter bank account.

At one point, I looked around my bathroom and realized I'd unintentionally started a museum of failed fixes. Half-used lotions, abandoned gadgets, expired powders. It looked like a graveyard of broken promises. I've probably spent thousands chasing cures for being human. The big revelation? None of it worked. And yet, the one product I always come back to? A $5 drugstore coconut lotion that actually makes me happy. It doesn't erase wrinkles, it doesn't change my life, but it smells like vacation in a bottle and that's more than any $95 miracle serum ever gave me.

The dumbest one I ever tried? A so-called "fat-melting belt." You strap it on, sit there, and supposedly watch the pounds melt away. I looked like a burrito wrapped in Velcro and just ended up sweaty in places no human should be sweaty. That wasn't a fix. That was a crime scene.

And it doesn't stop there. I once bought an "ionized water bottle" that promised to detoxify my body and boost my energy. You know what it did? Made my water taste like a nine-volt battery. Or the time I caved and bought "healing crystals" that were supposed to balance my hormones. I'm still sweating, still cranky, and now out fifty dollars.

Unfortunately, you can't buy your way out of being human. Stress, fatigue, aging, weight gain; it's all part of the deal. No cream, powder, or gadget is going to fix that. Sure, some things help a little, but the real fixes are free: sleep, water, laughter, and boundaries. All infinitely more effective than a burrito belt or a bottle of rocks.

Maybe the real miracle product is acceptance, the kind you can't buy online. Turns out peace doesn't ship overnight.

So next time you're tempted to hit "buy now" on something that swears it'll change your life, pause. Ask yourself: is this the answer, or just another expensive distraction? And for the love of all things decent, make sure they have a refund policy. Because the best fix isn't in a bottle. It's laughter, lowered expectations, and maybe a decent night's sleep.

Chapter 16: Menopause Madness

Menopause is like puberty in reverse. Only this time, there's no thrill of becoming an adult, just the joy of sweating through your clothes while forgetting why you walked into the kitchen.

Everyone tells you about hot flashes, but nobody warns you just how bad they really are. They also don't tell you that you'll start dressing in layers like an onion with commitment issues.

Flash makes it sound quick. Cute, even. Reality? It's a full-body, five-alarm meltdown that comes out of nowhere. One minute you're fine, the next you're peeling off layers in public like you're auditioning for a strip show you didn't sign up for. I've stood in front of the fridge at midnight, door wide open, just breathing like it was my own personal spa treatment.

And then there's the brain fog. One day you're sharp as a tack, the next you're standing in the pantry holding a bag of flour like it holds the secrets of the universe. Conversations derail mid-sentence. Keys disappear daily. And don't even get me started on trying to remember passwords. At this point, I'm convinced menopause and technology are in cahoots.

The emotional swings are their own carnival ride. One minute you're crying at puppy commercials, the next you're raging because someone left a spoon in the sink, and five minutes later you're laughing so hard you can't breathe. It's like your hormones are running a game show and you're just the contestant stuck on stage with no lifeline.

And let's not forget the hair. Oh yes, menopause blesses you with random chin hairs, as if hot flashes weren't enough humiliation. I once had one stubborn chin hair that refused to come out no matter how hard I tried to pluck it. I'd sit at my desk absentmindedly playing with it, convinced today would be the day. But when it came time for removal, it vanished. Gone. Like it had tunneled back into hiding, laughing at me. Then, of course, it would reappear at the worst possible time, usually in public, glinting in the sunlight like a disco ball for my personal shame. Honestly, chin hairs are the ultimate menopause prank.

I've spent thousands (yes, thousands) on supposed cures. Teas, supplements, herbal drops, yoga poses, breathing techniques. You name it, I've tried it. And guess what? Still sweating. Still foggy. Still occasionally crying because someone ate the last cookie. The only thing lighter was my bank account.

And let's not forget the nighttime joyride — insomnia. You're exhausted all day, but the second your head hits the pillow your brain decides it's time to rehearse every conversation you've ever had since 1994. By 3 a.m., you're wide awake, Googling whether night sweats can actually kill you, and by 7 a.m. you're dragging yourself out of bed like a zombie in yoga pants.

The funniest (and saddest) part is the advice people give. "Have you tried meditation?" Sure. I can't even sit still long enough to remember why I walked into the kitchen but let me try emptying my mind on command. Or "just dress in layers." Great idea, but at this point, my layering system looks like I'm prepping for a fashion show in hell: sweater on, sweater off, tank top, blanket, ice pack. Repeat.

And then there's the thermostat war. Ken is always freezing, I'm always melting. After years of negotiating, we finally compromised: the thermostat stays locked at 69 degrees year-round. He walks around the house bundled like he's preparing for an Arctic expedition, while I'm sprawled in front of the fan like a lizard on a hot rock. Somehow, when we crawl into bed at night, it works. We can still cuddle without me combusting or him freezing solid. That, my friends, is true love in the age of menopause.

Menopause taught me that resilience isn't pretty. Sometimes it's sweaty, emotional, and held together by sheer stubbornness, but it's still strength.

Menopause isn't a phase you "get through." It's a whole new season of life, and it's not glamorous. But it's survivable with humor, patience, and maybe a freezer stocked with ice packs.

Chapter 17: How to Find Joy Without Joining a Cult

Happiness has turned into a billion-dollar industry. Everywhere you look, there's a course, a program, or a retreat promising to unlock "true joy" if you just buy their package. If someone's charging you rent money to teach you how to smile in matching yoga pants, you're not joining a movement, you're joining a cult with a better website.

Joy isn't found in a subscription box, a juice cleanse, or a weekend seminar under fluorescent lighting. Joy isn't branded. It isn't curated. It doesn't need a trademark symbol.

Ken's idea of joy is a nap and a sandwich. No hashtags required. Honestly, he might be onto something.

Real joy is simple. It's coffee in the morning when the house is quiet. It's a dog who thinks you're a superhero just for walking through the door. It's slipping into clean sheets at the end of a long day. It's laughing so hard your stomach hurts. It's choosing not to answer the phone and realizing the world didn't end.

For me, joy is in the little things that don't cost a dime and don't need to be staged for Instagram. It's watching the sunset over the mountains, when the sky turns into a painting nobody could recreate. It's sitting around the fire pit on a cool night, wrapped in a blanket, letting the silence do all the work. It's just sitting, holding hands with Ken, no words needed. Because sometimes the best joy is simply being next to someone who makes the chaos survivable.

But somewhere along the way, people started chasing joy like it was a trophy. They sign up for retreats, buy matching mats, chant affirmations, and wait for the lightning bolt of happiness to strike.

Meanwhile, the rest of us are just thrilled when Taco Tuesday rolls around.

I once had a friend spend weeks stressing about getting tickets to a "life transformation" seminar. The cost alone could've paid for an actual vacation. Meanwhile, Ken and I were sitting on the porch drinking iced tea, laughing so hard we nearly fell out of our chairs. Guess who found joy that night? It wasn't the one chanting in a conference room.

Joy doesn't need to be bought, branded, or bundled into a six-week course. It doesn't need to look impressive on social media. Joy is in the small things, the ones nobody else notices. And if you're too busy chasing the next big promise, you'll miss the simple stuff that's already in front of you.

So skip the cult. Skip the overpriced retreats. Stop waiting for joy to arrive in a package. It's not hiding in a seminar room. It's in the everyday moments you're probably rushing past.

Joy's not hiding at a retreat center; it's sitting right beside you on a porch, maybe holding a taco.

Chapter 18: The Joy of Lowered Expectations

Somewhere along the way, we got tricked into thinking life had to look perfect. Spotless houses. Pinterest-worthy meals. Children who behave like catalog models. A career that makes you rich but somehow leaves time for daily yoga, homemade sourdough, and volunteering at the animal shelter.

Nobody is living like that. Not even the people posting about it on Instagram.

Lowering your expectations isn't failure, it's freedom.

The fantasy version of my house? A sparkling clean space that smells like fresh linen and looks like a magazine spread. The reality? A laundry mountain in the corner, dishes that multiply like rabbits, and at least one mystery smell I can't track down (more than likely the dog). Guess what? Nobody cares. People don't come over to inspect your baseboards. And if they do, they're not guests, they're inspectors.

Same goes for dinner. The fantasy version is a balanced, home-cooked meal with organic vegetables and love. The reality is cereal. Or takeout. Or cereal *and* takeout. And everyone lived. Lower the bar. Sometimes feeding people is the win, not impressing them with your ability to julienne carrots.

And let's talk about holidays. The fantasy is matching outfits, perfect family photos, and a table that looks like Martha Stewart herself styled it. The reality? Someone forgot the rolls, the dog stole the turkey, and the family photo looks like a lineup from *America's Most Wanted.* And you know what? Those are the moments everyone actually remembers. One year, our dog managed to drag the Christmas tree halfway across the living room before anyone noticed. Ornaments flew, the lights went dark, and the whole house looked like it had been ransacked by Santa's delinquent elves. We laughed until we couldn't breathe, and honestly, that memory has outlasted every "perfect" holiday photo. That's the good stuff.

Same thing with aging. We all start out thinking we'll be put together forever. Smooth skin, toned bodies, wrinkle-free foreheads. Then menopause shows up, gravity kicks in, and suddenly "put together" just means you found a clean shirt without stains on it. Lowered expectations don't mean giving up, they mean making peace with reality. And reality is a hell of a lot easier to live in than perfection.

When you stop competing with impossible standards, life suddenly gets lighter. You don't have to apologize for not being perfect. You don't have to apologize for being human. Perfection is exhausting. *Good enough* feels like a vacation.

That's the joy of lowered expectations. Not because you're settling, but because you're choosing sanity over stress.

The more I let go of how life 'should' look, the more I started to love the life I actually have.

Chapter 19: Everyone's Tired. Be Nice Anyway

It's a universal fact. Everyone is tired. Parents are tired. Workers are tired. Teachers, nurses, baristas, delivery drivers? All tired. Even the people who look like they've got it all together are running on fumes. Everyone's one missed nap away from chaos. Some of us are already there. Life is exhausting, and most of us are just trying to keep the wheels from falling off.

That's why kindness matters more than ever.

If your coffee order is wrong, it's not a personal attack. The barista isn't plotting against you. They're just trying to survive the morning rush without crying into the espresso machine. Show them some grace.

If someone's blocking the grocery aisle with their cart, maybe they're distracted by bills, stress, or just the weight of existing. Barking "EXCUSE ME" like a drill sergeant doesn't make you efficient. It just makes you an asshat. Trust me, as much as this is one of my personal pet peeves (move the cart, people!), I try to remind myself they might just be having a rough day. Annoyed? Absolutely. But patience beats turning into the villain of someone else's story. Be nice.

And if you've ever snapped at a cashier, only to realize later you weren't mad at them. You were mad at your own stress (you know what I'm talking about). I've done it. I've watched their face fall, felt that gut-punch of regret, and realized they didn't deserve the storm I brought with me. They were just the nearest target. That moment sticks with you. It should. Be nicer.

We're all carrying invisible loads. Some heavier than others. You never know who's one bad interaction away from completely breaking down. So why add to it?

Life is already hard enough. Bills, jobs, traffic, hot flashes, diets that don't work, friendships that fizzle, bosses who micromanage, jeans that betray you, medical diagnosis, it's plenty. The one thing that makes it worse is people being jerks on top of it.

Ken's motto for surviving it all is take a nap, eat a snack, don't engage with idiots. Works every time.

So don't be one. Don't be the reason someone else's day tips from bad to unbearable. Hold the door. Say thank you. Put the cart back. Drive like a decent human. Show up for your people. And when you can, laugh. Because laughter makes the hard stuff survivable.

That's it. That's the whole lesson. Be kind. Not because it's profound, not because it'll change the world overnight, but because it makes life just a little easier for the rest of us who are barely hanging on.

Kindness doesn't mean you aren't tired too. It just means you refuse to let exhaustion turn you into someone you aren't.

Kindness won't solve the world, but it keeps it livable.

Epilogue: In Conclusion, Don't Be That Person

If there's one thing life has taught me, repeatedly, dramatically, and sometimes with a little slap to the face, it's this:

Lowering your expectations doesn't mean lowering your standards for life. It means lowering your stress about life.

It means giving yourself permission to be human. It means letting the world be imperfect without letting that imperfection ruin your day. It means laughing when things go sideways instead of spiraling. It means choosing grace over rage, and presence over performance.

I spent years trying to be the perfect version of myself. I wanted to be the perfect mother, wife, woman, professional, friend, neighbor, and grocery-store customer who never blocked an aisle. And all it ever did was make me tired.

Exhausted, actually.

So I stopped. Not suddenly. Not gracefully. But slowly. By seeing the humor in chaos, the beauty in ordinary moments, and the peace in lowering expectations of perfection.

Life got lighter. Easier. Better. Not because circumstances changed, but because I did.

Lowering expectations allowed room for joy, real joy, to show up. Not the loud, dramatic, fireworks-in-the-sky kind. But the soft moments:

- Ken laughing at something ridiculous

- A sunset that takes my breath
- A tiny miracle disguised as intuition
- A quiet morning with a warm drink
- A day that didn't go perfect but still felt right
- The realization that the worst things didn't break me, they rebuilt me

When you lower the expectations that don't matter, you make room for the things that *do*.

Peace. Presence. Laughter. Kindness. Connection. Clarity. Self-respect. Love that feels steady and safe.

That's the real magic.

Because the truth is, the world isn't getting slower. People aren't getting easier. Life isn't suddenly going to turn calm and predictable.

But *you* can.

You can choose to be the soft place in a hard world. You can choose not to take everything personally. You can choose to laugh instead of combust. You can choose gentleness, with others and with yourself. You can choose peace in the middle of everyone's chaos. And you can choose to stop expecting everything — and everyone — to be perfect.

Lower your expectations of the nonsense. Raise your expectations of the things that matter. Let life be what it is: messy, weird, funny, painful, beautiful, ordinary, and miraculous all at the same time.

If you walk away from this book with anything, let it be this:

Life doesn't have to be perfect to be wonderful. Lower your expectations and watch everything get better.

And for the love of sanity…Be kind. Be gentle. Be human. And when all else fails?

Laugh. Lower the bar. And blame it on menopause.